This library edition published in 2015 by Walter Foster Jr.,
a division of Quarto Publishing Group USA Inc.
3 Wrigley, Suite A
Irvine, CA 92618

Distributed in the United States and Canada by
Lerner Publisher Services
241 First Avenue North
Minneapolis, MN 55401 U.S.A.
www.lernerbooks.com

First Library Edition

Library of Congress Cataloging-in-Publication Data

Torres, Jickie.
Robots / Story by Jickie Torres ; Illustrations by Bob Berry. -- Library edition.
pages cm. -- (Watch me draw)
ISBN 978-1-93958-138-9
1. Robots in art--Juvenile literature. 2. Drawing--Technique--Juvenile literature. I. Berry, Bob, 1953- illlustrator. II. Title.
NC825.R56T67 2015
743'.89629892--dc23

2013011685

012015
18582

9 8 7 6 5 4 3 2 1

Robots

Story by Jickie Torres
Illustrations by Bob Berry

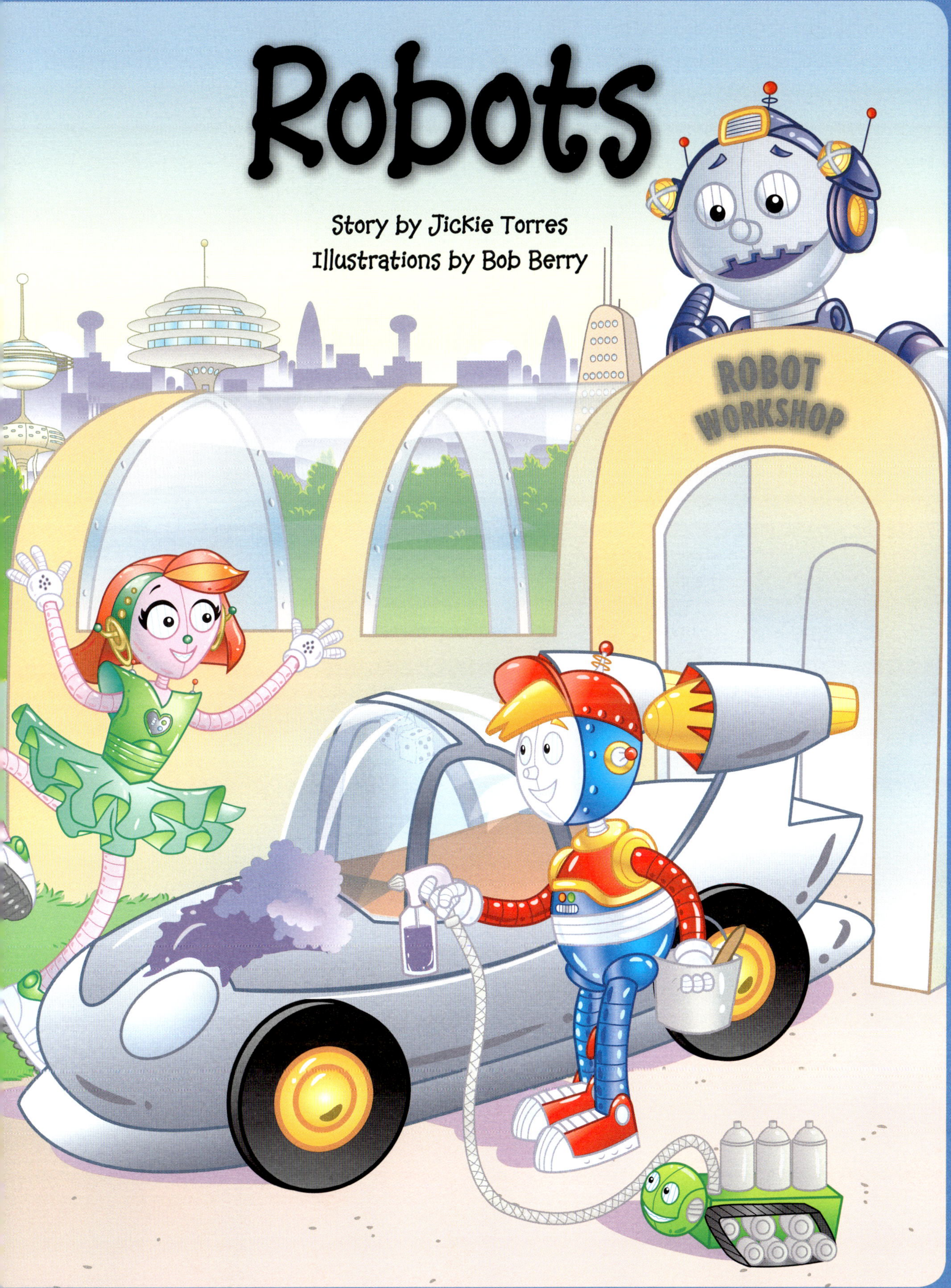

"I don't have much time!" said Bop the robot. "The space race is at one o'clock, and there's so much to be done." Bop looked around Robot Workshop. All of the robots were working happily. Bop wanted to find a quiet spot to concentrate—he needed to build the perfect racecar to help him win the race.

Draw Flash, the robot dog!

1

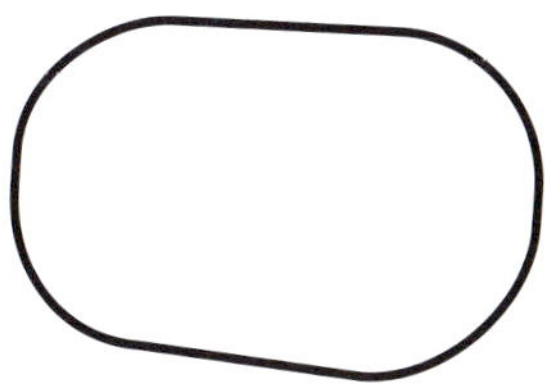

2

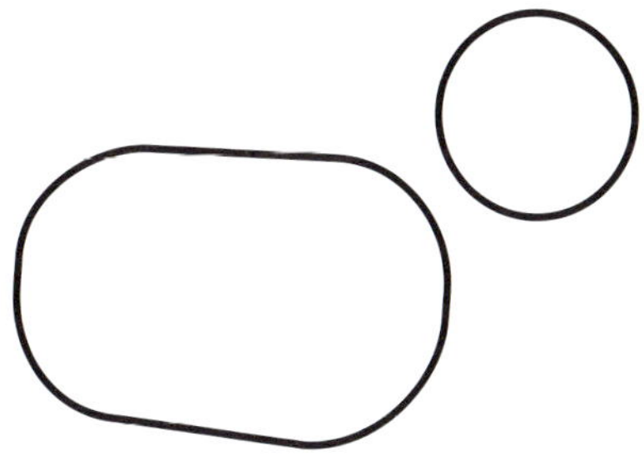

3

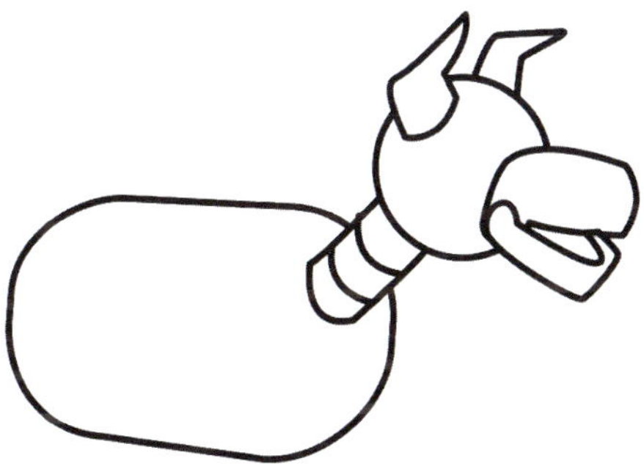

4

5

6

"Metal floor, check. Four tough tires, check," Bop recited aloud. Time was running out fast, but Bop had every part ready to go. He was just about to set the tires down when he heard a loud *whoosh!*

Draw the clock!

1

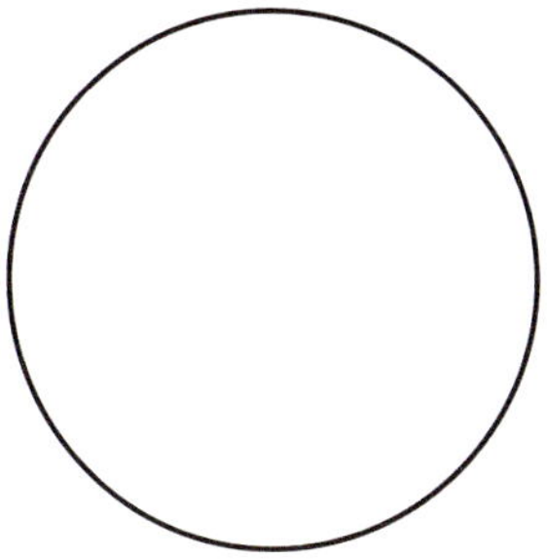

2

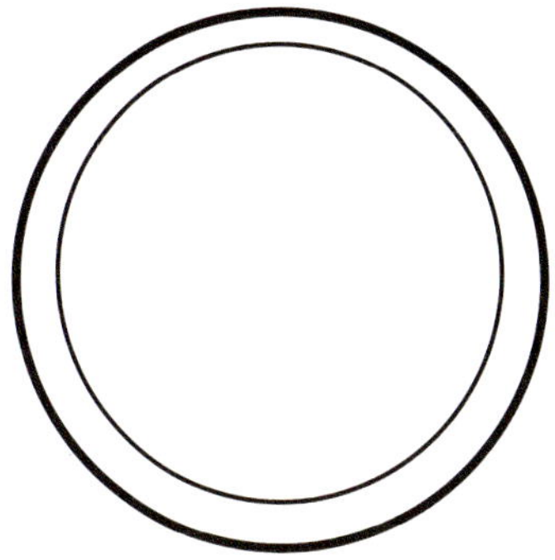

3

4

5

6

It was Twirl the robot, whirling into Bop's spot. Bop watched as his sketches went flying into the air. "Hey Bop!" Twirl said with a grin. "Whatcha workin' on?" Bop took a deep breath and picked up his papers. He patiently told Twirl about his plans for the race. "I bet I could help you build a racecar that'll surely spin you right into first place!" she said. "Um, thanks, but no thanks, Twirl. I've got this under control," Bop said.

Draw Springer!

1

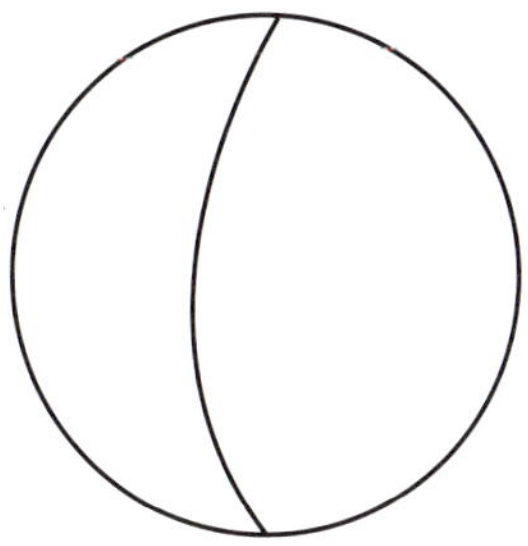

2

3

4

5

6

Things were coming together, and Bop was on a roll. But suddenly he felt a splatter. It was Art the robot. Art only meant to pat Bop on the back, but instead he splattered paint on the racecar door. "Art!" exclaimed Bop. "Hello and goodbye! Please, I must get back to work!" A sad Art rolled away. He only wanted to help.

Draw zip!

1

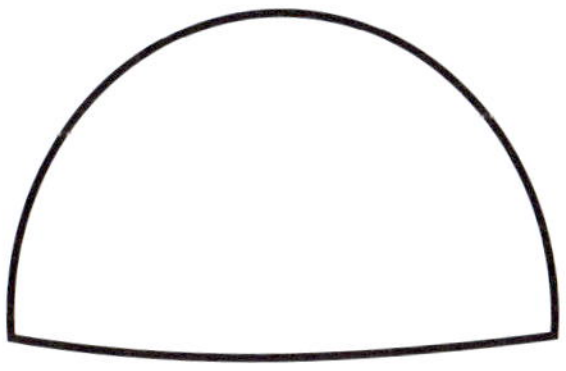

2

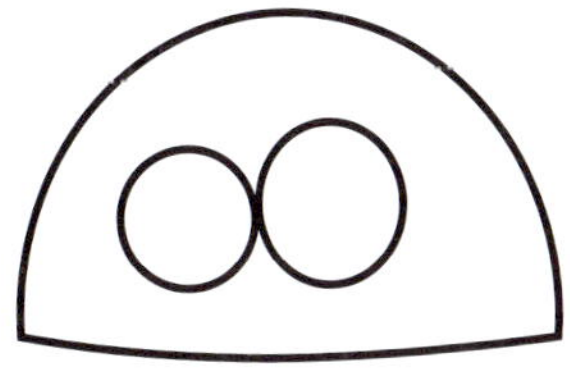

3

4

5

6

"Wow! Your racecar looks cool!" said Bit as she buzzed around Bop's head. Bop strained to get the gas pedal in place. "Thanks, Bit," said Bop as he struggled to get the screw on tight. "Is it fast? Is it tough? Are you going to paint it pink?" Bit asked excitedly. "Did you design it yourself? Was it hard? I hope you finish in time!"
"Biiiiiiit!" Bop shouted. "How will I ever finish with all of your questions?"
"Sorry," Bit mumbled sadly. She flew away and left Bop alone to finish in peace.

Draw Bit!

Bop pushed the racecar outside. He wanted to see if it sparkled in the sunshine.
"You've done a great job!" a deep voice boomed loudly behind him. It was Hugo, the biggest, strongest robot at Robot Workshop. He was casting a shadow over Bop's car.
"Hugo! You're in the way and now I can't see at all!"
"Oops, sorry Bop. I'll get out of your way," Hugo said.
"Good luck today."

Draw the flying car!

1

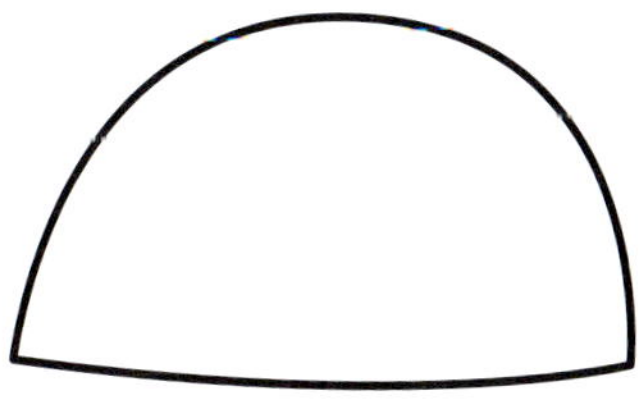

2

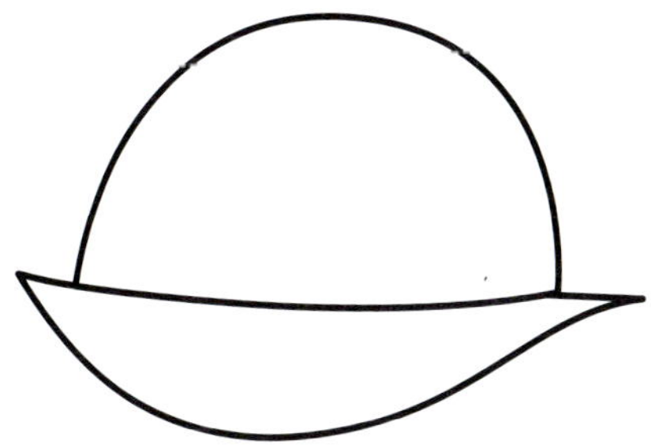

3

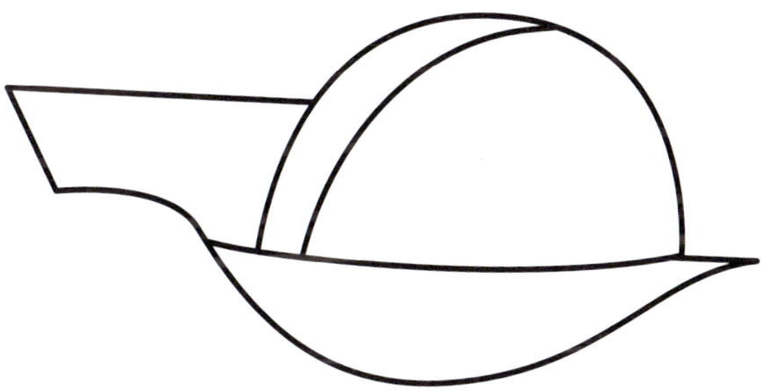

4

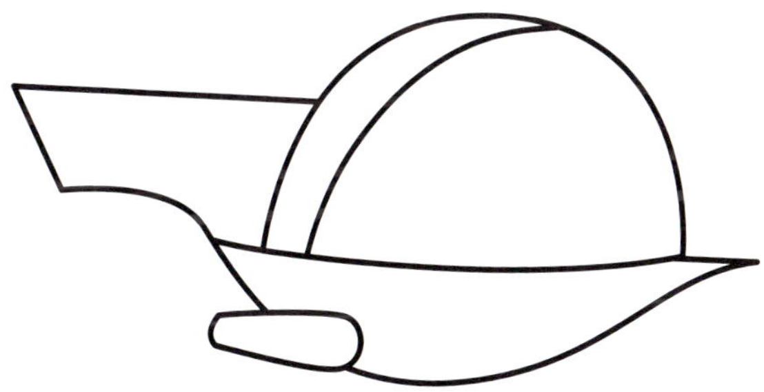

5

6

"Almost done," Bop said to himself excitedly. He looked up at the clock and smiled. He would finish just in time! Just then, Shakes ran over to see the fancy racecar she'd been hearing about all day. "Wow, Bop!" she said. "It looks super! I bet you're gonna win! I bet you're gonna win!" sang Shakes while she danced around in victory.

Draw Shakes!

1

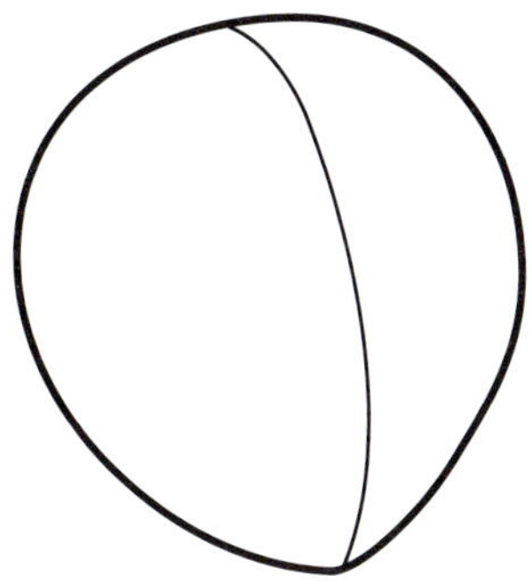

2

3

4

5

6

Hugo heard Shakes and ran out to join the celebration. Between Shakes's wiggling and Hugo's jumping, the ground began to rumble. Bop's beloved racecar started to fall apart! "Oh no, my car!" shrieked Bop. "It's ruined! It's broken! And all because of your crazy dancing!" Hugo and Shakes felt terrible! They hurried back inside the shop.

Draw Gig!

Bop looked sadly at his once magnificent car. It was quiet outside, except for the chirping of a cricket nearby. Bop was finally alone—just like he had wanted all along. But it wasn't as great as he thought it would be. He was lonely. And now he had no chance of finishing the car in time for the race.

Draw the cricket!

1

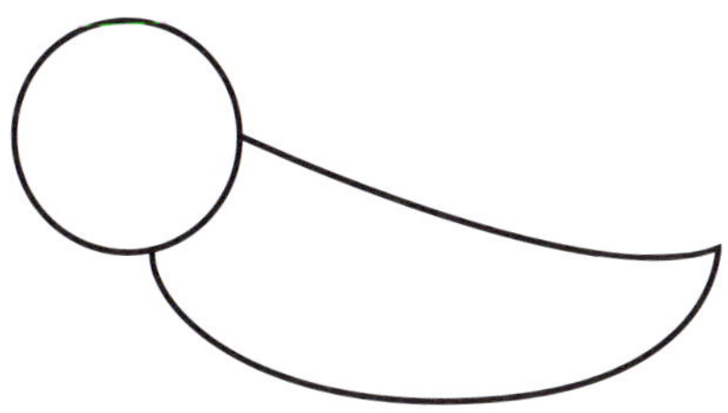

2

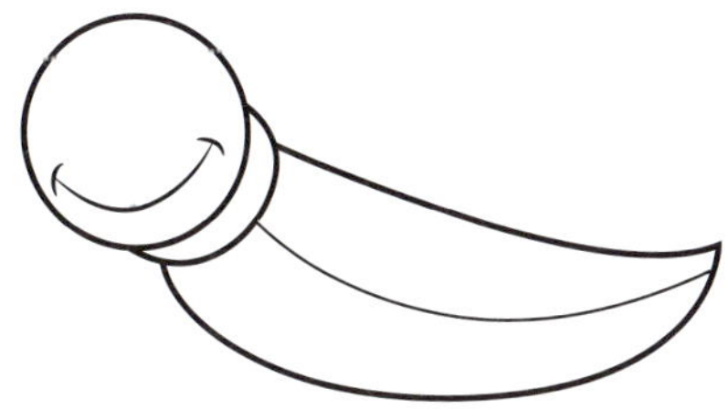

3

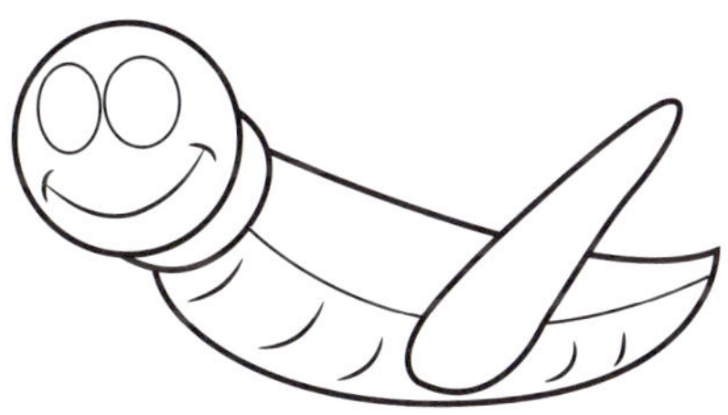

4

5

6

"Don't worry, Bop! We can help you put your car back together in no time," said Shakes. Twirl spun around like lighting and screwed each tire on. Bit fit easily beneath the steering wheel and put the pedals into place. Hugo held everything together while the robots worked. Bop was astonished.

Draw the tree!

"Hold on!" said Art rushing outside. "I've got the finishing touch." With a few quick strokes and a roll of his paint wheel, the car was like new again. "Could you add a lighting bolt?" asked Bop. And just like that, the car was finished. Everyone cheered. "Now off to the race!" Hugo declared. "Thank you all so much," said Bop. "Wish me luck! I wanna win for our team!"

Draw Bop's racecar!

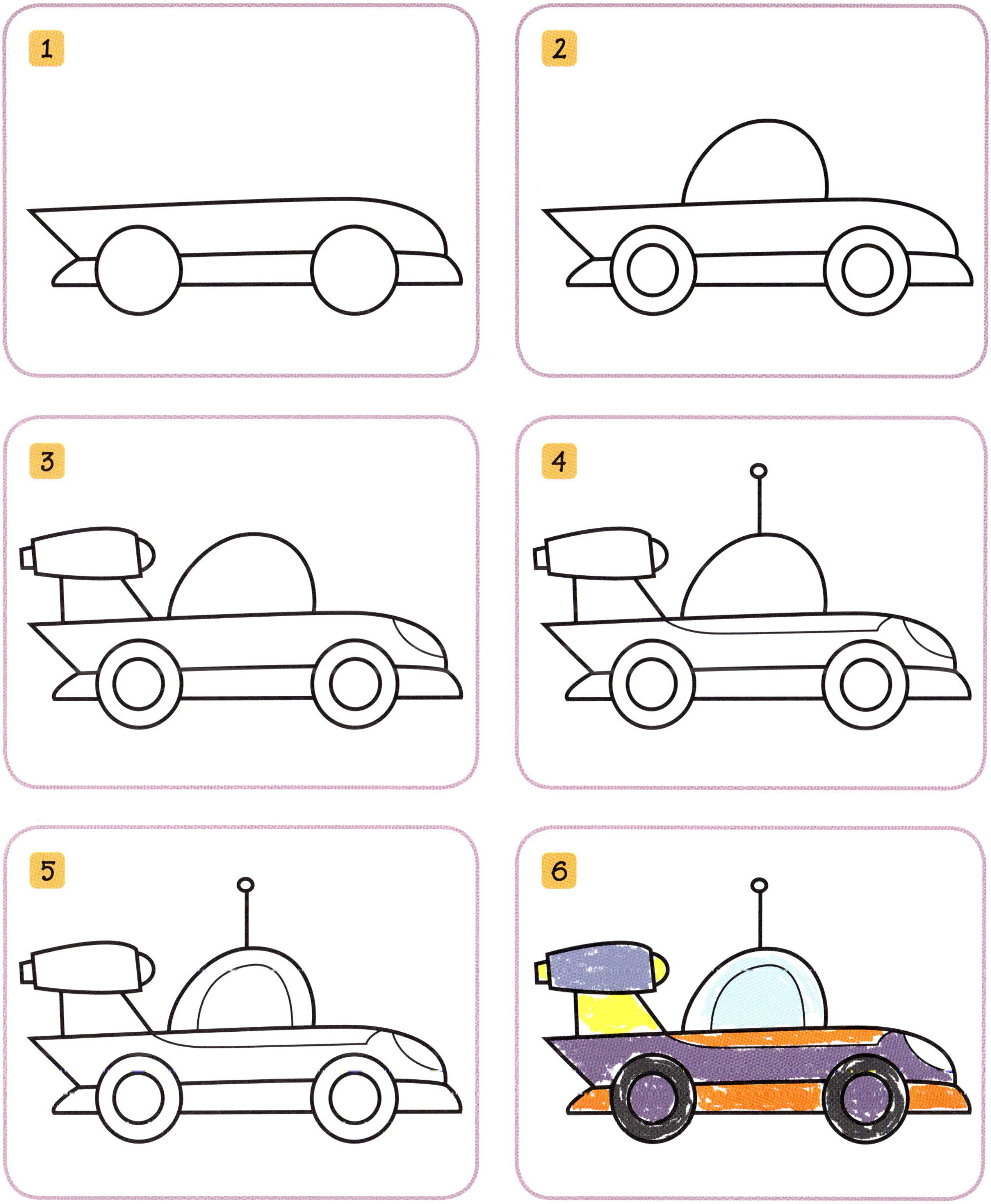

And just like that, Bop won the race—
thanks to a little help from his friends!